My Victory for God's Glory

A Book of Strength

My Victory for God's Glory:

A Book of Strength

By: *Krystal G. Williams*

My Victory for God's Glory
Published by Following His Way Publishing
Copyright © 2018 Author Krystal G. Williams.

All Rights Reserved.

Printed in the United States of America
ISBN: 978-0-9887188-4-5

Special discounts are available on bulk quantity purchase by book clubs, associations and special interest groups. For details email:
info@followinghisway.com.

Author Dedication

I would like to dedicate, **My Victory for God's Glory: A Book of Strength** to my Lord and Savior, Jesus Christ. To be given the ability to express myself through written poetry for the purpose of healing one's self, as well as others is such a tremendous gift and responsibility.

I am beyond thankful that God allowed my personal words to begin the healing process in my own life. There have been so many moments through the journey of writing this book that I have had to say to myself, *"it was good that I was afflicted."* God is the center and key of every piece in this book. To be chosen and used as a vessel to do the will of God is an honor that I will always respect and uphold.

To my family: my parents, Vernon and Barbie and my siblings, Trayon and Marcus, thank you very much for your love and support. You have traveled with me through the process of encountering and overcoming each challenge and hardship in my life, which in turn, gave me something to say in order to better myself as well as, those God would send to hear my truth, MY TESTIMONY.

Table of Contents

Introduction

My Victory for God's Glory: *A Book of Strength* is a collection of poetic devotional pieces that takes an in-depth look into the many facets of my life; exploring the areas of love, loss, joy, doubt, passion, forgiveness, hope, and the power of position.

Every poetic devotional herein was created with the sole intent of showing how God brought me through every challenge; allowing me to receive the victory for His glory.

It is my hope that, by reading these poetic devotionals, readers will gain three things:

1) an understanding that one is never alone throughout trials and tribulations,
2) life in its current state is not always what it looks like, and
3) if you give God the time and rest in patience, He will get the glory out of each and every area of your life.

My brothers and sisters in Christ, I hope that you enjoy!

1

There Is Always Hope

(Devotional # 1)

There is always hope.
Hope for a better, brighter tomorrow.
No matter how bad things can get,
there is always hope.
I have to hold on to this belief because it is the very
notion that keeps me going **STRONG**.

There is always hope.
I will be the one that makes it to the better side of
this ordeal.
If I have no other reason in the world to smile,
"there is always hope."
It gives me just a little something that turns my
frown upside down.

There is always hope.
I will not be dragged down by the hardships or trials
of life.

Because I honestly believe that my grasp on hope
gives me all the will-power I need to fight.
There is always hope.
So, when you feel like the four walls are closing in
on you, hold tight to hope and that will be enough to
successfully push and see you through.

Believe me…

There is always hope

Devotional Scriptures of Focus

Jeremiah 29:11 NIV-For I know the plans I have for you," declares the LORD, "plans to prosper you and not to harm you, plans to give you hope and a future.

Isaiah 40:31 NIV-but those who hope in the LORD will renew their strength. They will soar on wings like eagles; they will run and not grow weary, they will walk and not be faint.

Psalms 31:24 NIV-Be strong and take heart, all you who hope in the LORD.

Theme Term

Hope

Devotional Discussion Questions

1. What are some "things" that you are hoping for at this time in your life?

2. What actions are you implementing in order to make your hopes a reality?

3. Name two "things" that you hoped for in the past that have now become a part of your current reality?

4. What are some ways to increase spiritual
   strength and well-being?

My Sleeping Partner: A Testimony

(Devotional #2)

Now, I know you are probably
thinking to yourself, whatever,
she is about to share is about
The Lord, right? And, the answer
to this question is yes!
Yes, it is.

This piece will take you back.
Back to the place and time
where, I first had a one-on-One
experience with The Lord.
Where, I first knew that there was
something bigger than myself
watching over me. That special thing
that made me believe.

Every believer has this experience
that I am speaking of.
However, every experience offers up a different
situation, location, time, and feeling.
Mine however, happened to take place in a
townhouse that I rented, up in the second-floor
bedroom, in a bed where I tossed and

turned battling with the fears of facing the next
morning.

As I laid my head on a pillow
soaked in my own tears with
the feeling of my heart being broken
into a million and more pieces.
I began to wonder to myself,
"How did I get here?"
Here to a place of depression and grief.
I thought this move was suppose
to make life better.

You know, set me on the path of making
something of myself. This journey
was supposed to feel good or so I
thought to myself, as I forced
my face in to the pillow and let out a
scream. A scream that held on to
the absence of love that I was feeling,
the mistreatment I was receiving,
and the knowledge that I
had brought it all on myself.
That very night, Jesus,
yes, Jesus became my sleeping
partner. I remember it just
like it was yesterday.
Once my screams failed to make
a sound and my tears got tired of
falling, I wrapped myself in a cover
and curled up in a ball.

Speaking out loud with no one to hear
and answer me back, I said,
"There has to be more to my life.
God, I need to know that You are real
I need to know that You see what
I am going through.
Jesus, please make it better.
Please help me get some sleep because
if You don't, I won't have enough to
make it through."

And, I am telling you with confidence
that, that very night Jesus became
my sleeping Partner. As I begun
to fall asleep, I could feel myself being
held and loved like never before.
The next morning, I woke up
with the feeling that I knew
God was real and that
the Savior had come to see about me
and not only did He come and see
about me, but He also took the time
to hold me to sleep.
He came when I needed Him the most.
He allowed me to rest in Him.
I know with all my heart that having Jesus as a
sleeping Partner saved my life. That very night set
me on a journey that I will forever travel to serve the
Savior Who came to help and hold me to sleep.
My sleeping Partner.

Devotional Scriptures of Focus

Exodus 33:14 NIV-The LORD replied, "My Presence will go with you, and I will give you rest."

Psalms 4:8 NIV-In peace I will lie down and sleep, for you alone, LORD, make me dwell in safety.

Philippians 4:6-7 NIV-Do not be anxious about anything, but in every situation, by prayer and petition, with thanksgiving, present your requests to God. And the peace of God, which transcends all understanding, will guard your hearts and your minds in Christ Jesus.

Theme Term

Rest

Devotional Discussion Questions

1. Describe in detail, your first spiritual experience with God as your Protector.

2. When was the last time you devoted one-on-One time to building your spiritual relationship with God?

3. What are a few coping skills that you apply when you feel burdened, confused and/or depressed?

I am Stronger Than Before: (The Victory in My Testimony)

(Devotional #3)

I am stronger than I used to be.
So much stronger than before
I am no longer being swallowed
up by life itself.

I no longer lose sleep to fears and doubts
that seem to eat away at the eight hours I have
allotted for rest with every twist and turn that I
make.

My strength no longer allows me to fall victim to the
tears I let fall deep into my pillow and the loud
screams I let out in silence.

See, I am no longer walked on by the world.
The negative whispers of so-called friends,
and the lack of belief put forth by family
members just doesn't mean that much!

I have even learned to cast down my own
negative thoughts about self!

I am now even more than I think.
I can do more than I believe.

I am so much stronger than before.
However, I must be honest and
let you know, this self-growth did not come with
ease...
It has taken great time and patience.
I had to learn that my strength
comes from God and God alone.

And, in Him, I am more than a conquer.
I am only stronger than I used to be
because I now have a stead-fast, unshakeable
relationship with the Creator that took His time to
create me.

A Book of Strength

Devotional Scriptures of Focus

Philippians 4:13 NIV-I can do all this through him who gives me strength.

Isaiah 40:29 NIV-He gives strength to the weary and increases the power of the weak.

Ephesians 6:10 NIV-Finally, be strong in the LORD and in his mighty power.

Theme Term

Strength

Devotional Discussion Questions

1. As you look back over your life, what is one specific area where you believe you have grown stronger?

2. What two areas of weakness and/or fear would you like to strengthen this year?

I Thought They Took Away My Name

(Devotional #4)

This loss!
A loss that held so much power
my very being seemed to be
stripped away by force.
A force that has completely taken
my breath away.
Like the rug had been pulled right from under
my plan of life

I thought they took away my name
I fail to know who I am…
What I am made of…
Do I have what it takes to survive such a lack?
Covered in pain and whipped by the thoughts
of doubt and insecurity.
Robbed!
I have been robbed by their actions!

Actions that have caused such a change…
A change that I was not prepared for.
Any sort of preparation would have been
better than the surprise of losing all that I am

I thought they took away my name because

I thought they gave me purpose
I thought they gave me reason
I thought they gave me fight
I thought they made me someone

As I take the time to give my thoughts some thought
and, how I have given "them" and "they" the ability
to wreak havoc on my concept of self, I have come
face-to-face with the stronghold – **people bondage**!

Trapped by their ever-changing views.
Incarcerated by my need to be accepted.
Thinking that they were my only way.
Who knew that the very loss that brought
me to my knees in the beginning would set
me free in the end.

"Them" and "they" are just "them" and "they."
I am the child of the Most High God.
And, before Him there will be no other
So, call me Favored!

Devotional Scriptures of Focus

Job 10:12 NET-You gave me life and favor, and your intervention watched over my spirit.

Psalms 30:5 AMP-For His anger is but for a moment, His favor is for a lifetime. Weeping may endure for a night, But a shout of joy comes in the morning.

Exodus 33:12 NIV-...You have said, 'I know you by name and you have found favor with me.'

Theme Term

Stronghold

Devotional Discussion Questions

1. Do you currently have any strongholds at this time? If so, what are those strongholds?

2. How are you working toward freeing yourself from the stronghold(s) listed above?

3. What techniques do you practice on a daily basis in order to maintain your high self-esteem and/or to build up your self-esteem?

More Than a Smile

(Devotional #5)

It is so much more than a smile
that you see on my face.
It is the gateway to my internal joy.
The smile that you see now flashes
across my face to show that
I have made it based upon my own standards.
I am no longer a hostage to my own inner
limitations and battered by the opinions of the
world.

It is so much more than a smile
that you see on my face.
My grin shows the power that exists
within me. A power bestowed upon me by the
KING of all Kings.
I am smiling because there is nothing
too big for me to achieve.
I feel like I can walk across the
deepest, darkest sea.

Yes, it is so much more than a smile
that you see on my face.
I have finally become strongly
connected to the hero that has always
lived inside of me.
Overcoming the pain and anger
that once had the ability to destroy me.

I am no longer a victim
but a winner that is proud,
proud to display her great victory.
Can't you see by the beautiful smile
that now fits so perfectly?

Devotional Scriptures of Focus

2 Corinthians 12:10 NIV- That is why, for Christ's sake, I delight in weaknesses, in insults, in hardships, in persecutions, in difficulties. For when I am weak, then I am strong.

Isaiah 12:2 NIV- Surely God is my salvation; I will trust and not be afraid. The LORD, the LORD himself, is my strength and my defense; he has become my salvation."

2 Timothy 1:7 NIV- For the Spirit God gave us does not make us timid, but gives us power, love and self-discipline.

Theme Term

Perseverance

Devotional Discussion Questions

1. How do you maintain your internal joy throughout life's many ups and downs?

2. List three "things" that make you smile daily?

3. Discuss one situation that once distressed you that you can now smile about?

4. What does happiness look like to you?

All the Pressure On You

(Devotional #6)

I put all the pressure on you.
You were supposed to come in and save me.
Heal all the wounds created by a life before you.
Your validation gave me worth and value.

See your "You are beautiful"
Made me beautiful.
Your "You are smart"
Made me smart.

And, your "I love you"
Made me someone to love.

I put all the pressure on you
To keep me happy,
Fill my heart with joy,
Shield me from all harm,
Erase all the insecurities.

I depended on you to protect me from myself.
You became my idol.
You became my air.
The life that I desired to live.
Yes, I was your one-woman army, ready to defend.

All praises for the woman that I was belonged to
you. I put all the pressure on you...
Without ever thinking that you would fail me
Or the weight would be too much.

See, I gave a man, a human all the power and ability
that belongs only to our GOD!
I put all the pressure on you.

Devotional Scriptures of Focus

Psalms 118:8 NIV-It is better to take refuge in the LORD than to trust in humans.

Psalms 146:3 NIV-Do not put your trust in princes, in human beings, who cannot save.

Hebrews 13:8 NIV-Jesus Christ is the same yesterday and today and forever.

Matthew 19:26 NIV-Jesus looked at them and said, "With man this is impossible, but with God all things are possible."

Theme Term

Pressure

Devotional Discussion Questions

1. Do you believe in "Me" time? If so, how do you like to spend time with yourself?

2. How can you continue to build upon your independence as an adult?

3. List some ways in which you can better prioritize your time daily.

God Is Up to Something Good

(Devotional #7)

God is up to something good.
What is about to spring forth
has brought about a true transformation.
A change in the way that I think.
A makeover in the way that I carry myself.
A shift in how I implement my faith.

Oh, God! My God is up to something good.
I can feel it deep down in my spirit.
This good thing that is about to come to
pass is more.
More than I could have ever imagined.
More than I could have ever hoped for.
More than I could have ever had the heart
to ask for.
My God, won't HE do it!
And, I do not even know what HE is doing.

My God is up to something good.
I have this feeling!
A feeling that makes me burst out
in tears of joy and thanksgiving.
A feeling that makes me offer up
a praise of "Hallelujah!"

Some would say, "you are shouting
without reason because I have nothing
to show for it."
BUT, I say that I am shouting with reason
because something is on the way.

My God is up to something good.
Thank You, God, for preparing a blessing
that I would not have enough room to receive.
Thank You for giving me a gift that I hoped for.
Thank You for giving me a blessing that only
the good Father can.

God is up to something good.
And, when it all comes to full manifestation,
I will say that I knew that God was up to
something good.
But even before it all happens, thank You
in advance.

A Book of Strength

Devotional Scriptures of Focus

Isaiah 22:22 NIV-I will place on his shoulder the key to the house of David; what he opens no one can shut, and what he shuts no one can open.

Galatians 6:9 NIV-Let us not become weary in doing good, for at the proper time we will reap a harvest if we do not give up.

Ephesians 3:20 NIV-Now to him who is able to do immeasurably more than all we ask or imagine, according to his power that is at work within us...

Theme Term

Patience

Devotional Discussion Questions

1. What do you believe has been one of your greatest transformational phases and/or processes in the past?

2. What does it mean when one begins to shift their way of thinking?

3. List four prayers/blessings that you are believing God for at this current time?

God Loves Me Through "NO!"

(Devotional #8)

All of my life I have held on to the belief
that God shows His love by saying, "YES" to His
children.

Through the process of growing,
 I have come to truly learn of God's Love
through the impact of His answer, "NO!"

After trying to force open doors,
close doors too soon,
manipulate false ideas of love,
and, living in a world of denial
I have come to know that a "NO" from God is
one of the greatest gifts you could ever receive.

It is the one gift that can shield you from heartache,
protect your temple from harm,
cover you from the struggles of obtaining a blessing
prematurely,
prolong when you still need time to grow
and, save your life all at once.

Oh, how He loves me so very much.
He took the time to say, "NO"
and, to make sure that I have heard Him well.

He is a great Father protecting and guiding His child.
His love is strong and unconditional.
The type of love that will allow me to be
uncomfortable and shed tears for a moment
only to make sure that I have lasting joy and laugher
in times to come.

See, God says "NO" to ensure that all things will
work together for my good.
So, I now take the time to appreciate the power and
tender care behind God saying,
"NO" just as I do when God says "YES!"

Devotional Scriptures of Focus

Romans 8:28 NIV-And we know that in all things God works for the good of those who love him, who have been called according to his purpose.

Isaiah 55:8-9 KJV-For my thoughts are not your thoughts, neither are your ways my ways, saith the LORD. For as the heavens are higher than the earth, so are my ways higher than your ways, and my thoughts than your thoughts.

Theme Term

Protection

Devotional Discussion Questions

1. What doors (relationships/
   situations/circumstances) has God protected
   you from by closing them?

2. What doors:
   (opportunities/promotions/relationships) has
   God blessed you through by opening them?

3. List three ways in which saying, "no" may be
   difficult for you?

He's Making A Way

(Devotional #9)

No, I do not see it.
No, I have no knowledge
of what direction it may come.
Nothing in my spirit is pulling
me either way.

My mind has no thoughts of
what may be ahead of me.
But, He is making a way.
It has been awhile.
The wait has not been easy.
Remaining steadfast and focus
has come with severe combat.

There are times where I grow tired.
Having to encourage myself
from letting go of hope
because I know He is making a way.

Yes, I know it does not look like it.
In fact, I may at the moment look like
the biggest fool. But,
I know He is making a way.
Having to remind myself that God
will come through.

But, how do I know?
How am I so sure?
Confident in the fact that God will show
up for me…
I know He is making a way because I know
He did not bring me to this place of uncertainty
to leave me here.

He will bring me through in His own
time and way.
Watch!
Keep your eyes open.
Pay close attention.
And, before you and I both know it,
I will be provided with the way that He was making
because I know He is making a way.

A Book of Strength

Devotional Scriptures of Focus

Exodus 14:13-14 NIV- ..."Do not be afraid. Stand firm and you will see the deliverance the LORD will bring you today. The Egyptians you see today you will never see again. The LORD will fight for you, you need only to be still."

Psalms 23:1-3 NIV-The LORD is my shepherd, I lack nothing. He makes me lie down in the green pastures, he leads me beside quiet waters, he refreshes my soul. He guides me along the right paths for his name's sake.

Psalms 91:14-16 NIV- "Because he loves me," says the LORD, "I will rescue him; I will protect him, for he acknowledges my name. He will call on me, and I will answer him; I will be with him in trouble, I will deliver him and honor him. With long life I will satisfy him and show him my salvation."

Theme Term

Journey

Devotional Discussion Questions

1. Are there times in your journey as a believer where you have grown impatient? If so, please explain those specific moments.

2. What are some specific ways that you encourage yourself while awaiting God's will to unfold in your life?

3. What are some special ways in which God has shown up and made a way for you?

Calling Me Out

(Devotional #10)

God, I can hear Your voice softly saying my name.
You are calling me out.
Calling me out of what I perceive to be normal.
My way of living life.
My security; dysfunctional security.
This life, this place, this moment I have accepted
with ease.

You are calling me out.
Calling me out of my familiar nature into
inexperienced land.
Being one that always needs to be in the know.
Your calling me out alters the plan of course I
thought my life should take.

You are calling me out
How did You know that I truly required more?
How did You know that I truly was made for more?
How did You know that I truly desired to be more?
Your calling me out is something that my soul
cannot deny but, my mind fights.
Now physical rest does not come easy.
Constantly pacing the floor.
Thoughts racing…

You are calling me out.
I am beginning to wonder…
what this call will bring.

Wanting to experience all that this call has placed
upon my life.
This call is changing everything and all of me
Thank you Lord for knowing that I needed to be
called.
You are calling me out!

A Book of Strength

Devotional Scriptures of Focus

John 15:16 KJV-Ye have not chosen me, but I have chosen you, and ordained you, that ye should go and bring forth fruit, and that your fruit should remain: that whatsoever ye shall ask of the Father in my name, he may give it you.

1 Thessalonians 5:24 NIV-The one who calls you is faithful, and he will do it.

Theme Term

Calling

Devotional Discussion Questions

1. Do you believe that The Lord has called you? If so, what is your calling in this life?

2. Has there ever been a time in your life where you battle with the call of The Lord on your life?

3. In your opinion, is there a difference between being called and chosen by The Lord?

It Didn't Kill Me

(Devotional #11)

No, it didn't kill me.
I am still here.
I am still breathing
It didn't completely take me out.
I'm a little surprised myself.
in the midst of the storm,
the circumstances themselves
were supposed to wipe me out clean
but, I am still here.

More than a little cut-up
and no shortages of bruises, somehow
the scars don't look that bad.
It didn't kill me.
Chest caving in from pain
but, my heart still beats at a slow, but steady pace.

Cerebral damage from mental wars
with many defeats under my belt.
But, my mind still, still belongs to me.
I didn't lose it in the process.
It didn't kill me.

It may have hurt me to my core.
Knocked me off balance a bit.
Caused me to take some steps in pure fear.

But, it didn't kill me.
And, it won't
because I still have purpose,
that is why I am still here.

A Book of Strength

Devotional Scriptures of Focus

Ezekiel 37:12-14 NIV-... 'This is what the Sovereign LORD says: My people, I am going to open your graves and bring you up from them; I will bring you back to the land of Israel. Then you, my people, will know that I am the LORD, when I open your graves and bring you up from them. I will put my Spirit in you and you will live, and I will settle you in your own land...'

Psalms 23:4 KJV-Yea, though I walk through the valley of the shadow of death, I will fear no evil: for thou art with me; thy rod and thy staff they comfort me.

Psalms 27:13-14 NIV-I remain confident of this: I will see the goodness of the LORD in the land of the living. Wait for the LORD; be strong and take heart and wait for the LORD.

Theme Term

Overcome

Devotional Discussion Questions

1. Discuss one moment in your life where you felt defeated?

2. Discuss one challenge you have encountered in life that you believe God fought on your behalf?

3. What are two scriptures that you rely on to prepare for a spiritual battle?

Slow Walk

(Devotional #12)

I am going to do this at a different
pace. I will slowly walk this thing out
if I have to. Letting go of the desire
to be just like the rest.
To do as they do,
when they do as they do,
and why they do what they do,
will no longer be a concern of mine.

Allowing the trends, achievements,
traveled territory, or the approval
of others to control my every step
will no longer be permitted.

I will slowly walk this thing out.
Their opinions, comments, likes
and dislikes can be discussed between
them alone. I am not in need of their
blueprint to help me find my way in
in my own life.

This life that I live may include many
but functions only off of the foot
steps of one. I will continue to let them
travel at the speed of light. It is well
with me if you pass me by and attain
the things that I still only wish for.

I will slowly walk this thing out
Taking the process one step at a time.
Obtaining and reaching each and every
level when I, myself am good and ready to.
Many say that life is passing me by.
Some believe that I am stuck or at least
should be so much further.
I myself hold tight to the internal
and repeated pull that keeps me in line
every time I try to move a little too fast
for my own good.

As I slowly walk through life's journey,
I am learning to listen to the desires of
my own heart, to build upon the woman
I am steadily becoming, to appreciate
and take hold of the fact that my steps
are not ordered by my counterparts
But by God, Himself.

Devotional Scriptures of Focus

Joshua 1:5 NIV-No one will be able to stand against you all the days of your life. As I was with Moses, so will I be with you; I will never leave you nor forsake you.

Joshua 1:9 NIV-Have I not commanded you? Be strong and courageous. Do not be afraid; do not be discouraged, for the LORD your God will be with you whenever you go."

Matthew 28:20 NIV-...teaching them to obey everything I have commanded you. And surely I am with you always, to the very end of the age"

Theme Term

Process

Devotional Discussion Questions

1. What is more important to you as a believer, the process or the promise?

2. Have you ever experienced a time where you felt that it was you and God against the world?

My Soul-Mate

(Devotional #13)

I am having a hard time.
A very hard time trying to pinpoint every facet
and I do mean every facet that connects me to you.
It is clear, I know you're there somewhere.
You just have to be.

Because I can feel, hear, and see your presence.
It is like the ever so frequent visions of you give
me...
Gives me something to want, push, and battle for.
Our spirits became one long before either one of us
could have ever given acknowledgement to the term
soul-mate.

I dream of a life with you replaying in my head
as though I am living it today.
It feels so real! Oh, you are less than a touch away
Songs remind me of our everlasting love
Movies re-enact the growing chemistry that exist
within this bond
Because you are my soul-mate
you breathe life into my everyday actions.

Can you feel, hear, and see my presence?
Look, I smile just to give you hope.
I inspire to learn just to give you the power of
knowledge.

It is my overall duty to execute your desires because
only I can.
It makes me proud to share my soul with the mate
of a lifetime.
Taking me higher than the greatest possibilities.
Helping me become the best me ever with your love.

But, it all means nothing...
Nothing at all, if I am the only one that believes and
yearns...
Yearns for this type of love.
Are you really my soul-mate? - OR -
A strong soul-tie used by the enemy for the purpose
of distraction? – OR-
Just preparation of a new season yet to come?

Devotional Scriptures of Focus

1 Corinthians 13:4-8 NIV-Love is patient, love is kind. It does not envy, it does not boast, it is not proud. It does not dishonor others, it is not self-seeking, it is not easily angered, it keeps no record of wrongs. Love does not delight in evil but rejoices with the truth. It always protects, always trusts, always hopes, always perseveres. Love never fails.

2 Corinthians 10:3-4 KJV-For through we walk in the flesh, we do not war according to the flesh...

Ecclesiastes 3:1 NIV-There is a time for everything, and a season for every activity under the heavens...

Theme Term

LOVE

Devotional Discussion Questions

1. Do you believe in the term soul-mate?

2. What is your definition of love?

3. How has your definition or view of love changed and/or developed since becoming a believer?

Fear ~or~ Change

(Devotional #14)

Change has never been a friend of mine
In fact, it has played the role of my most
dangerous enemy.

I am one that has never needed to explore
anything that travels beyond the limits of
my comfort zones.

A safety net is so much more than a safe guard
put in place just in case something may go
wrong, it is the very shield that controls the
way in which I live.

Terrified to step out into the unknown, I have
encased myself into the routine of all I have
ever known. Telling myself the lie that I don't
long to experience more. When the truth is that fear
and its sidekick failure have taken away my
opportunity to take hold of anything new.

And then, comes the pull of change. This pull
has caused such a mental battle that my entire
body tries to walk away from. This pull of change
throws me into the idea that there is so much
more life available unto me and that my best
self is yet to be uncovered. Filling my head
with the hint of anything better than being

here. But wait, I thought, here was safe.
Here was comfortable and change…
Change is the enemy. That is what the fear
of failure reminds me before I can even make
the first step.

As I try to quiet my own thoughts, I come to
understand that change is something I will
never achieve on my own. If I want to be
anything more than what I am at this very
moment, I will have to surrender my fears
and failures unto The Lord and say, "have
Your way and please lead the way."

Devotional Scriptures of Focus

Psalms 56:3 NIV-When I am afraid, I put my trust in you.

Psalms 119:105 NIV-Your word is a lamp for my feet, a light on my path.

Luke 1:37 KJV-For with God nothing shall be impossible.

2 Timothy 1:7 NET-For God did not give us a Spirit of fear but of power and love and self-control.

Theme Term

Change

Devotional Discussion Questions

1. Does the process of change come easily to you or is changing more of an internal battle?

2. How have you allowed fear to impact your way of life?

3. What is one thing that you have given fear permission to steal from you?

I Loved So Hard

(Devotional #15)

I loved so hard, from beginning to end
The way that I loved completely blinded me
I was unable to see anything
Red flags
Lies
True interest
Even the pain that the lack of sight
caused me.

I loved so hard
that I began to zone out from the world.
Who did I call outside of you today?
Time passed me by as though it never existed.
Daily conversations with a few of my closest friends
used to mean the world to me.
Now, I was comfortable with being
cooped up in a box where your face and voice
was all I needed to make it through my day.

I loved so hard
that I forgot what made me truly smile.
I could no longer remember what gave me passion.
I lost my voice and ability to stand up for myself.

I loved so hard
that you had become my lord.
Someone that could do no wrong.

Even if I didn't want to face it,
you became the very thing that I worshipped.
However, you did not create me.
The power that I gave to you had to be taken back.

I loved you so hard that
I completely forgot about
the God that breathed life into me.

No one should ever love that hard...

A Book of Strength

Devotional Scriptures of Focus

Exodus 20:3 NIV-"You shall have no other gods before me.

Psalms 37:4 NIV-Take delight in the LORD, and he will give you the desires of your heart.

John 3:16 NIV- For God so loved the world that he gave his one and only Son, that whoever believes in him shall not perish but have eternal life.

Theme Term

Self-Worth

Devotional Discussion Questions

1. In what ways do you believe you have devalued yourself for the sake of another?

2. What are your relationship red flags and deal-breakers?

3. How do you display self-appreciation and value?

Love Shown Through a Limp

(Devotional #16)

An affliction that has taken hold of me
from the moment I failed to reach
and successfully pass the developmental
milestone of walking.

To place one foot in front of the other has
never and I do mean NEVER come with ease
Pounded by my inability to function properly
placed a target on my head, labels on my back
and threw damaging blows to my self-esteem.

See growing up, I thought like the town's people in
the book of John. Whose sins brought such a curse
upon my body? For years, I went on a search to find
someone to blame for my shortcomings, physical
pain, and my loss of a chance to be considered
normal.

In my eyes, someone needed to pay for forcing me
to have to overcompensate in every other area of my
life because I failed to stand up straight and just
walk.

Something that looked so simple and came with ease to everyone else caused me such great agony.

Mentally, I developed an inadequate view of myself all because of what I lacked physically. I wrapped myself up in the whispers of thoughts like:
You are abnormal
Something is wrong with you
You will never fit in
How will you survive in a world you cannot keep up with?

My own tormenting thoughts caused me to cover myself in the sadness of having to live
with a curse that I thought was sure to last a lifetime.

And then, came Forest Grump. Yes, Forest Grump!
I wanted to be like Forest so much.
If running from the negative words of others, the degrading thoughts of self and the unknown future could have only set me free. I would have run my days away.
But, I am not Forest. No, I am not!
My journey would lead me a totally different route.

So, lets fast-forward to the point I thought I was surrendering it all; when I first believed. You know, when you first discover that you are loved by the Most High God and that Jesus died for you?

But, let's be honest, I started with the mentality that God was my Santa Claus. Well, at least until I became acquainted with Paul. I thought that I was

the only one to pray for God to remove an affliction
from my life He continued to allow me to keep.

Oh, but how my relationship has begun to change
and flourish. In the days, months, and years to come
God would show me how much He loved me
though my limp. I know now that I am not cursed
BUT blessed and highly favored. The Lord started
my life off with a testimony, from the day I was
born.

If you ask me today, my limp is one of the greatest
gifts I could have been given. God allowed me to
function with my limp in order to set me apart, to
cause me to have to call on Him and come to Him,
and to slow me down just enough so that I could
truly see what this life has to offer.

See I had no other choice but to learn to fight my
fight with His strength and run my own race at His
pace.

My good ole limp has provided me with a special
skill set. I can see pain through the biggest smile,
understand living with not enough, and loving
people for who they are, right where they are.

I have picked up my bed and, I am walking with it.
For His grace is sufficient and, I am forever thankful
that God has shown His love through my limp.

Devotional Scriptures of Focus

2 Corinthians 12:9 NIV-But he said to me, "My grace is sufficient for you, for my power is made perfect in weakness." Therefore, I will boast all the more gladly about my weaknesses, so that Christ's power may rest on me.

Psalms 119:71 NIV-It was good for me to be afflicted so that I might learn your decrees.

Theme Term

Affliction

Devotional Discussion Questions

1. What areas of your life can you look back and say, "It was good that I was afflicted?"

2. In what ways do you believe afflictions help to produce blessings?

3. In what ways has God's grace been sufficient in your life?

Everything That You Need (Letter of Encouragement)

(Devotional #17)

Dear My Child,

I have given you everything
that you need.
Listen.
No, truly listen and
take in all that I am saying,
I have given you everything
that you need.

Yes, I know where you have
fallen short.
I understand the limits you
have set for yourself.
I remember your childhood
and, I know you feel short-changed.
I can accurately recall all that has been
said and done to you.
I even know how frighten you are.

But, please hear Me,

I have given you everything
that you need.
You are more than prepared!
Called for such a time as this!
Built to withstand.
Structured to make a lasting difference
and, blessed to produce good fruit!

I have given you everything
that you need to become who you are destined to be.
Nothing you have gone through in the past,
may be going through in the present, or
will go through in the future
will ever stand in the way of My plans for you
Because I have given you everything
that you need.

Please trust and believe in Me!

Love,

God
Your Father!

Devotional Scripture of Focus

Ephesians 6:13-17 NIV-Therefore put on the full armor of God, so that when the day of evil comes, you may be able to stand your ground, and after you have done everything, to stand. Stand firm then, with the belt of truth buckled around your waist, with the breastplate of righteousness in place, and with your feet fitted with the readiness that comes from the gospel of peace. In addition to all this, take up the shield of faith, with which you can extinguish all the flaming arrows of the evil one.

Theme Term

Equipped

Devotional Discussion Questions

1. What special life skills do you believe God has equipped you with?

2. If you took the time to write a letter to God, what would it say?

How Do I Forgive?

(Devotional #18)

How do I forgive all that has been done?
I know that I am supposed to,
It is my moral duty, right?
I just do not feel strong enough.

They all say I should humble myself.
Wow! Yeah that really sounds easy.
But the wounds are still so tender, and
at the slightest touch, my heart cries
out in pure pain.

How do I forgive?
They say time heals all.
But I am not sure if there is
a measurement of time that could completely
erase my hurt; the hurt that stops me right in
my tracks at every thought.

How do I forgive?
When I still feel like I have a right to be
angry, no, **furious**!
I tell myself that I will not let this go with ease.
Someone must feel my burden.
I will not be the only one traveling through this
storm.

How do I forgive that which has not been asked to
be forgiven?
I have come to learn that through it all,
"How do I forgive?"
has become one of the most profound questions
I have come to ask.

No matter how hard I try to fight it,
by grace and mercy, I am learning to forgive
what I once thought was the unforgivable.
I am learning to say, "thank you" to the creators
of my wounds, pains, anger, and tears.

For they have now become my greatest professors in
this class called, "Life".
I now know and understand that I must forgive
in order to be forgiven for my many, many wrong-
doings.

I want to regain my power and life back from the
mountains of sadness.
So, yeah, maybe they were all right; I can really say
that I truly
Forgive you…
Now, let my real healing process begin!

Devotional Scriptures of Focus

Mark 11:25 NIV-And when you stand praying, if you hold anything against anyone, forgive them, so that your Father in heaven may forgive you your sins."

Matthew 6:14-15 NIV-For if you forgive other people when they sin against you, your heavenly Father will also forgive you. But if you do not forgive others their sins, your Father will not forgive your sins.

Theme Term

Forgiveness

Devotional Discussion Questions

1. Do you believe you have to forgive others in order to be healed yourself?

2. Discuss some wrong-doings you would like to be forgiven for.

3. Discuss some wrong-doings you would like to forgive others for.

If I Knew Then What I Know Now

(Devotional #19)

At some point in life, every
individual will find themselves
either saying or thinking,
"If I knew then what I know now."
Those exact words flowed from
my mouth so effortlessly as I
gave my mind permission
to travel back in time.

If I knew then what I know now
I would have never allowed myself
to get so imprisoned by my own
formulated plans, leaving no
flexibility for modification.
I am more than sure I would
have never permitted that
beautiful degree that I have
hanging on my wall to be viewed
as my source; the basis of my
identity. I am more than a major
and a grade point average.

If I knew then what I know now,
I would have removed the rose colored

glasses early in life. Everything is not
always what it looks like. I would have
never allowed my body to be misused
for the purpose of obtaining and keeping
what I thought was love. Just needing to
be validated by someone.

If I knew then what I know now,
I know for a fact that depression
would have never had a chance
to get such a tight grip on me
because I now know that life does
actually get better. I would have been
more selective in who I allowed in.
Who I called a friend. Now, realizing
that I hung as close to my own Judas
as Jesus did to His.

If I knew then what I know now,
I would have protected my heart
and mind. This protection alone
would have led to less broken pieces
lost that I am trying to find and put
together again. I would have aimed to
be more like my mother and respected
being covered by my father.

If I knew then what I know now,
God would have always been the center
of my life, my Love, my Friend, my Protector,
my Shelter, and my Healer. To tell the truth,
having a relationship with God is the only

reason why I know what I know now.
The wisdom that comes along with being
Born again.

A Book of Strength

Devotional Scriptures of Focus

Hosea 4:6 NIV-my people are destroyed from lack of knowledge.

Proverbs 1:7 NIV-The fear of the LORD is the beginning of knowledge, but fools despise wisdom and instruction.

Proverbs 2:6 NIV-For the LORD gives wisdom; from his mouth come knowledge and understanding.

Theme Term

Knowledge

Devotional Discussion Questions

1. What are some "things" that you wish you knew then that you know now?

2. How has your knowledge of God changed your life?

3. What are some words of wisdom you would like to share with others?

Your Kingship
Forgotten

(Devotional #20)

Someone forgot to tell you that you were a KING.
You have immersed yourself into the ways and
customs of the people of the world.
Wrapped yourself in the behaviors of the
commoners that want no more than what has been
handed down to them. Like a peasant, you have
clothed yourself in lack.

Failing to see who you truly are…
The man you are…
The leader that lives inside of you…
Your kingship has been forgotten.
And yes, as a child, someone forgot to tell you that
you were a KING.

You fail to take the position as head of the
household; the position that can bless many
generations to come.

You continue the cycle, following the paths of men
who failed to pick up their crowns and place them
on their heads.

Recognizing that they have been put in place to
protect, provide, and share the knowledge that only
a man can embody.
Your forgotten kingship has affected your wives,
sons, and daughters.

Tell me...
Who is going to tell your wife that her back is
covered when the burden is too heavy to bear?

Who is going to show your son the way he is to
follow?
The difference between a boy and a man...
A daddy and a father...
A leader and a follower?

Who is going to tell your daughter that she is a
princess that will one day wear the crown of a queen
and deserves to be treated as such?
What true love looks and feels like before she says,
"I do?"

Your kingship has been forgotten.
Someone has forgotten to tell you that you are a
KING.

You have forgotten how to lead the way.
Now, you are following in the footsteps that lead
nowhere. Picking up ways and agreeing to beliefs
that goes against your very essence.

God has provided you with so much wisdom.
Jesus has given up His life for you.
You have been adopted into son-ship.
You are an heir to God.
Viewed a little less than an angel...

Yes, your kingship has been forgotten.
However, it is never too late to let the old things
pass away.
Now, at this very moment, you can begin to claim
your crown. My KING!

A Book of Strength

Devotional Scriptures of Focus

Romans 8:14-15 NIV-For those who are led by the Spirit of God are the children of God. The Spirit you received does not make you slaves, so that you live in fear again; rather, the Spirit you received brought about your adoption to son-ship.

Romans 8:17 NIV-Now if we are children, then we are heirs—heirs of God and co-heirs with Christ, if indeed we share in his sufferings in order that we may also share in his glory.

Psalms 8:4-6 NIV-what is mankind that you are mindful of them, human beings that you care for them? You have made them a little lower than the angels and crowned them with glory and honor. You have made them rulers over the works of your hands; you put everything under their feet...

Theme Term

Position

Devotional Discussion Questions

1. What does a King look like through your eyes?

2. Identify the Kings in your life.

3. Identify some traits of a man that signify he has forgotten his Kingship?

The Weeping Willow

(Devotional #21)

My very being has become nothing more
than a bundle of great sadness.
My tears are so constant that the streams
that they leave behind have now washed away
the once found glow of my beautiful complexion.
The water that now departs from my eyes
have swept away the only hope that once held tight
to my soul.

It seems like I am drowning in my own sorrow.
Just look at the weeping willow.
My cries have now become the sum total of me
and that is all that they can see.
To the point where I can no longer picture a greater
reality.
Is this my destiny?

To get lost in the bitterness that I have allowed to be
brought upon myself.
Oh, poor weeping willow, everyone passing by feels
so sorry for me.
I have taken the enchanting glares away...
Away from everything around me.
Turning cold the beauty that dwells on both sides
and behind me.

And now, all I wish is that this weeping willow
would just…
Hide deep down inside of me instead of coming
out…
Out for the whole world to see.

Devotional Scriptures of Focus

Psalms 30:5 NIV-…weeping may stay for a night, but rejoicing comes in the morning.

Psalms 30:11 NIV-You turned my wailing into dancing; you removed my sackcloth and clothed me with joy…

James 1:2-3 NIV-Consider it pure joy, my brothers and sisters, whenever you face trials of many kinds, because you know that the testing of your faith produces perseverance.

Theme Term

Overwhelmed

Devotional Discussion Questions

1. Do you believe in using weeping (crying) as a way to release?

2. List some times in life where you feel the most burdened or overwhelmed?

3. What are some ways you've dealt with and overcome stressful situations that has proven to be effective?

You Are The Blessing

(Devotional #22)

I am pretty sure that you do not know
exactly who you are. And, it is an
honor and pleasure to let you know
that you, yes you, are the blessing.

The blessing that someone out there
has consistently asked God for.
Prayers have been placed upon the
throne for your very existence.

You are the blessing.
How can you not see that your words
are being used to lift the most burdened
spirits and that your drive gives the tired
soul the push that they need to make it
through? Your fight lets the greatest of warriors
know that there is still something worth fighting for.

You are the blessing.
Can you see, they are watching the way in which you
worship? They recognize that the praises that you
send up, changes the atmosphere. You have an
anointing that the most seasoned believers long for.
To connect with the Father the way in which you do
is something special.

You are the blessing.

As I confidently recited my opinion of whom I thought her to be. She softly asked, well, did you know that you were a blessing? And, all I could say was, "WHO, ME?"

Devotional Scriptures of Focus

1 Thessalonians 5:11 NIV-Therefore encourage one another and build each other up, just as in fact you are doing.

Luke 6:31 NIV-Do to others as you would have them do to you.

Matthew 5:16 NIV-In the same way, let your light shine before others, that they may see your good deeds and glorify your Father in heaven.

Theme Term

Encouragement

Devotional Discussion Questions

1. What does it mean to be a blessing?

2. Can you name three individuals that you view as blessings in your life?

3. What are some ways that you try to be a blessing to others?

Just A Little While Longer

(Devotional #23)

Hold on,
tight if you must.
Concentrate on what is to come.
You are too close to give up and
throw in the towel now.
Just a little while longer.

You have what it takes to keep
pushing against the odds.
I know you can't see your way through.
I know it can be challenging to step out on faith.
I know it may seem like you are standing on
the sidelines watching the
growth, acceleration and manifested blessing of
others.

Just a little while longer.
Just wait a little while longer.
Your blessing will come.
The appointment that you have been waiting to
receive.
The healing that you require.
The exposure you have been preparing for.
The love that you deeply desire is on the way.

If you could only see it then, you would know that
complete restoration is right around the corner.

Just a little while longer.
Hold on.
Tight if you must.
Because at the perfect time, every promise of
God for your life shall come to pass.
Just give your blessings a little while longer.

Devotional Scriptures of Focus

1 Corinthians 2:9 KJV-But it is written, Eye hath not seen, nor ear heard, neither have entered into the heart of man, the things which God hath prepared for them that love him.

Habakkuk 2:3 NIV-For the revelation awaits an appointed time; it speaks of the end and will not prove false. Through it linger, wait for it; it will certainly come and will not delay.

Jeremiah 29:11 NIV-For I know the plans I have for you," declares the LORD, "plans to prosper you and not to harm you, plans to give you hope and a future.

Theme Term

Patience

Devotional Discussion Questions

1. Does it get challenging to watch others receive their blessings while you are still in the process of waiting? If so, why?

2. Are you excited about the blessings that have been prepared just for you? What blessings are you thanking The Lord for in advance?

3. Write down three scriptures that you read and/or recall frequently to encourage yourself while you're on a patience walk?

And He Still Wants to Use Me

(Devotional #24)

God still wants to use me.
I just do not understand why
God still wants to use me.

There are times where my faith
can move mountains and then,
there are times where I
do not even have enough faith to
keep hope alive within myself.

Why would You want to use me?
Sometimes I fail to have the faith
and determination like Joseph,
willing to lean on the will
of my God at any cost.

There are instances where I only
have my ears open to the things that
make me comfortable. Lord, why
would You use me?

I struggle with instruction.
I battle with doubt.
I hide from the unfamiliar.

I can be controlled by my fear.

Why would You want to use me
out of all those that could be used?
And, yet, He still wants to use me.

A Book of Strength

Devotional Scripture of Focus

Proverbs 3:5 NIV-Trust in the LORD with all your heart and lean not on your own understanding…

Theme Term

Chosen

Devotional Discussion Questions

1. Are there times where you feel unworthy to be used or chosen by God?
   ☐ Yes   ☐ No

Why?

Fighting Against My Own Mind

(Devotional #25)

My Mind
It's mine, I thought it belonged to me.
Until, the day my own thoughts
started to turn on me.
The battle of trying to keep it
together has finally taken its toll.
The struggle to hold on to my own
mental capacity has become a fight I
was never prepared to take part in.

What's going on?
How did this happen?
How did I lose my mind?
Thoughts racing and begging for
a tangible solution.

What day
What hour
Where
Did I decide to let it all go?

All the many questions truly mean nothing
because in God's perfect timing,
He decided to give it back.
The hedge of protection is secure!

A Book of Strength

Devotional Scripture of Focus

Romans 12:2 NIV-Do not conform to the pattern of this world, but be transformed by the renewing of your mind.

Philippians 4:7 NIV-And the peace of God, which transcends all understanding, will guard your hearts and your minds in Christ Jesus.

2 Corinthians 10:5 KJV-Casting down imaginations, and every high thing that exalteth itself against the knowledge of God, and bringing into captivity every thought to the obedience of Christ.

Theme Term

Clarity

Devotional Discussion Questions

1. What are some coping strategies you implement to combat confusion, depression, and/or anxiety?

2. Please discuss one situation that has challenged you mentally and emotionally?

3. List two scriptures that you use and recall in a time of need for help, comfort or support?

It Is Here

(Devotional #26)

The day has finally come.
I am living in my answered prayers.
Your will for my life is truly coming to pass.
In this position of now, I sincerely know that
You were listening.
You heard my cries.
The silent groans that I failed to put into words.

You were paying close attention to it all.
The day has come.
Where the blessings are no longer still
being prepared.
I am no longer in a position of hoping
for that which I cannot see.

I am no long wondering if my prayers ever
reached Heaven's ears.
I can more than see the wonders of The Lord
for my life.
I am living graciously in the full
manifestations of that God has promised me.
It is here!

Devotional Scripture of Focus

Ecclesiastes 3:1 KJV-To everything there is a season, and a time to every purpose under the heaven...

Ecclesiastes 3:11 NET-God has made everything fit beautifully in its appropriate time...

Theme Term

Timing

Devotional Discussion Questions

1. Have you ever given up on a blessing that you were waiting to come to pass? If so, explain.

2. What are some "It Is Here" blessings that you have received in your life?

A Book of Strength

The God of My Hard Places

(Devotional #27)

As I sit here and battle within my own mind.
Do I have enough energy to make it through…?
Through a battle that I never thought in my life
I would have to fight.

I feel like I am fighting for my life…
My life!
Not my finances.
Not a man used for a mere purpose of filling
an internal void.
Not friends taking up space for the purpose of
having someone to say, "I agree with you."
But my life. I never knew how important health
could be to your overall destiny.
And that struggle to say,
"Thy will be done"
when you are not even sure what
God's will is for your life.

The bombardment of doctors and reports that
you are fighting hard not to believe.
God has become the God of my hard places.
The places where I decided not to eat or sleep.

Where I know if I gave my thoughts any more
thought my mind may no longer be mine.

When you know that God did not give you the spirit
of fear but the fear is so strong that you are
wondering how did the enemy come in and just take
a seat?
I heard a preacher say once,
"How do you know God is a healer if you have
never been sick?"
I can openly say that I never really knew the power
of that very statement
until, I needed a healer myself.

However, to be completely honest, although the
fight has not been easy, God has provided provision
every single step of the way.
I know he sees me as good and he is ordering my
steps somewhere.

Fighting for my life to be back like…
How it used to be.
How I use to feel.
But God is saying, no, I have more for you.
I am not taking you through this process to
put you back into the same position again.

It is more than healing on the way.
It is complete restoration on the
other side of this fight.
And, I am about to win!

A Book of Strength

Devotional Scripture of Focus

Deuteronomy 31:6 NIV-Be strong and courageous. Do not be afraid or terrified because of them, for the LORD your God goes with you; he will never leave you nor forsake you."

Isaiah 41:10 NIV-So do not fear, for I am with you; do not be dismayed, for I am your God. I will strengthen you and help you; I will uphold you with my righteous right hand.

Psalms 34:17-18 NIV-The righteous cry out, and the LORD hears them; he delivers them from all their troubles. The LORD is close to the brokenhearted and saves those who are crushed in spirit.

Theme Term

Fighting

Devotional Discussion Questions

1. Have you ever felt like you were in a battle for your life? If yes, explain.

2. What does "The God of My Hard Places" mean to you?

3. Have you ever struggled with whose report to believe over your life or current situation? If yes, explain.

So, I Waited for You

(Devotional #28)

So, I waited for you.

I knew that you would come.
In my spirit, I knew that there was
a you that existed out there somewhere in the
atmosphere.

The Savior, my Lord reminded me on a daily basis
that if I truly gave myself over to Him that He would
give me the desires of my heart.

So, I waited for you.
To say, I waited rolls off my tongue easier
than the experience of the process itself.
See, minutes turned into days,
and days turned into weeks,
and weeks turned into months,
and months turned into years.

How in the wait, life had started to pass me by.
Making an idol out of you.
Becoming to blind to focus
How could you...
A you that I did not know take the place of the
God who created me.
Distracted by my desire.

Distant from my true purpose.
Waiting in my own strength became too much for
me.

But, I waited for you.
I would tell myself it is going to get easier.
However, the course of the road did not change
until, I realigned myself with the real reason for the
wait.

So, I waited for you but I really was not waiting for
you.
To be honest, I did not tell them:
Do not touch me like that.
I do not want to drink.
I do not belong in this place.
I do not do those things anymore
because of you,
I did it all for who God was calling me to be.

So, I guess after all this time, I have been truly
waiting for me.
But because I serve a good God, once I become
who and what He has destined me to be,
you will be the gift that I receive.

Devotional Scripture of Focus

Matthew 6:33 NIV-But seek first his kingdom and his righteous, and all these things will be given to you as well.

Genesis 29:20 NIV-So Jacob served seven years to get Rachel, but they seemed like only a few days to him because of his love for her.

Romans 8:24-25 NIV-For in this hope we were saved. But hope that is seen is no hope at all. Who hopes for what they already have? But if we hope for what we do not yet have, we wait for it patiently.

Proverbs 18:22 NIV-He who finds a wife finds what is good and receives favor from the LORD.

Theme Term

Transformation

Devotional Discussion Questions

1. If single or married, how has building a relationship with The Lord impacted your view on your personal relationships?

2. If single, how has your personal relationship with God aided in the process of waiting for love?

3. If married, how has your individual relationship with God helped in becoming one with your partner?

4. Do you believe in God "ordained" mates?

To Remain Steadfast

(Devotional #29)

I love God with all that is within.
However, there are times where
I struggle to remain steadfast.
Steadfast in my faith.
Steadfast in believing in the
promises of God.
Steadfast in knowing God has
a future designed just for me
and, that I am forever loved by the
LORD of all lords.

I am stable in all of my knowledge
when things seem to be going well.
Where the path traveled has no hills,
twists, turns, or bumps in the road!
My faith is solid as a rock then.
It is times where I have no clue
of what is going on around me.
Where, I have to come face-to-face with chaos.
The times when I do feel alone and forgotten.
Where having strength to endure is something of the
past.

I am trying so hard to remain steadfast.
I can't keep blaming the battle of double mindedness
on the human in me.

So, today, I will fight the good fight of faith with the weapon of knowing God will never leave nor forsake me.

A Book of Strength

Devotional Scripture of Focus

Joshua 23:8 NLT-Rather, cling tightly to the LORD your God as you have done until now.

1 Samuel 12:21 KJV-And turn ye not aside: for then should ye go after vain things, which cannot profit nor deliver; for they are vain.

1 Corinthians 15:58 NIV-Therefore, my dear brothers and sisters, stand firm. Let nothing move you. Always give yourselves fully to the work of the Lord, because you know that your labor in the Lord is not in vain.

Theme Term

Unshakable

Devotional Discussion Questions

1. In your opinion, what does it mean to remain steadfast unto The Lord?

2. What are some areas in your life where you struggle to remain focused and steadfast?

3. What distractions do you believe have a major impact on your relationship with God?

Given Dreams

(Devotional #30)

There once was a time where all
I could do was dream.
I thought that anything in my
personal will-power was possible.

Captivated by my ability to get
caught up in a vision of so much more…
More than my current reality.
Until, the moment real life hits.

I find it so amazing that no matter how
BIG your vision is for yourself, there are
days, events, points in time, moments in life
that tend to slowly tear away at your perfectly
created future.

These times seem to be purposely placed between
you and your hope for greater.
Managing to remind you that even the possible
can be a mere fantasy.
Until, God steps in and intentionally shows me His
will for my life.

Giving me the true desires of my heart
which are so much more than I could
have ever dreamt or imagined.

Devotional Scripture of Focus

1 Corinthians 2:9 NIV-However, as it is written: "What no eye has seen, what no ear has heard, and what no human mind has conceived"—the things God has prepared for those who love him.

Job 17:15 NIV-where then is my hope—who can see any hope for me?

Psalms 119:105 NIV-Your word is a lamp for my feet, a light on my path.

Matthew 6:10 NIV-your kingdom come, your will be done, on earth as it is in heaven.

Theme Term

Desires

Devotional Discussion Questions

1. Discuss specific desires that you believe God has placed on your heart?

2. What actions, views, and customs have you freely let go of since becoming a believer?

In the Breaking

(Devotional #31)

In the breaking
The pieces…
My pieces are forming a masterpiece.
The potter's wheel is turning.
As the wheel spins
I begin to lose control.
Control of what?
What I thought was…
Normal
Acceptable
Prefect
Right

Trying to fight to hold on to dear life
Dear life, really?
The life I have been living
has been no dear to me.
Every moment has setup the foundation
for the breaking…
My breaking.
I am broken but I am still here.
I recognize that it is time to
embrace the fact that I have been
shattered all over the place.
But, with my potter's guidance
My obedience

My willingness
to endure the process I will...
I will come forth as pure gold.
Even in my breaking!

Devotional Scripture of Focus

Jeremiah 1:5 NIV-"Before I formed you in the womb I knew you, before you were born I set you apart; I appointed you as a prophet to the nations."

Isaiah 64:8 NIV-Yet you, LORD, are our Father. We are the clay, you are the potter; we are all the work of your hand.

Ephesians 2:10 NLT-For we are God's masterpiece. He has created us anew in Christ Jesus, so we can do the good things he planned for us long ago.

Theme Term

Masterpiece

A Book of Strength

Devotional Discussion Questions

1. Do you remember the first time you knew God was taking time out to restore and heal you?

2. In your opinion, what does it feel like to be on the potter's wheel?

Dear, Curiosity

(Devotional #32)

Dear, **Curiosity**:

My darkest hours have let me
know that my Maker will never
leave nor forsake me.

So, please believe me when I say,
that is WHY I am still here with
life to live!

Signed the wisdom of a **SURVIVOR**!

A Book of Strength

Devotional Scripture of Focus

Exodus 14:14 NIV-The LORD will fight for you; you need only to be still."

Isaiah 40:29 NIV-He gives strength to the weary and increases the power of the weak.

Isaiah 41:13 NIV-For I am the LORD your God who takes hold of your right hand and says to you, Do not fear; I will help you.

Theme Term

Covered

A Book of Strength

Devotional Discussion Questions

1. Discuss some of your darkest moments in life.

2. How did you overcome the events discussed above?

3. Do you view yourself as a survivor?

I Am Number 8 As Well

(Devotional #33)

I came across a sermon preached by
Pastor, John Gray entitled: I Am Number 8.
Before I could even finish listening to the
words that he spoke, I begun to lift my
4s to the sky.
For I am number 8 as well.
For God to lead me to such a powerful
word at such a time shows just how
much of a loving Father he truly is.

Spending the last few months battling the
effects of my own type of Saul.
Feeling lost and broken, battered, and defeated.
Aware of the fact that I am viewed last in the sight
of man,
God has sent someone as I wipe my tears from my
sore cheeks to tell me that I too am number 8.

My lack of acceptance makes me someone.
The pain that I feel at this current time is
building my character.
Not knowing exactly where to go is allowing
God the freedom to lead the way.
My hidden existence is about to give

God some glory.

He is going to make something out of me.
No matter what it looks like right now,
I am my own kind of David,
and soon I will rise.
Not in my own strength or
by the will of man but because
God says it is time…
For I am number 8 as well!

Thank you so very much Pastor Gray!
And to God be all the glory!!!

A Book of Strength

Devotional Scripture of Focus

Proverbs 18:15 NET-The discerning person acquires knowledge, and the wise person seeks knowledge.

Isaiah 11:2-3 NIV-The Spirit of the LORD will rest on him--the Spirit of wisdom and of understanding, the Spirit of counsel and of might, the Spirit of the knowledge and fear of the LORD.

Proverbs 20:15 NIV-Gold there is, and rubies in abundance, but lips that speak knowledge are a rare jewel.

Theme Term

Inspiration

Devotional Discussion Questions

1. Can you recall one sermon that made an impact on your life while confronting difficult circumstances?

2. Name a few preachers, ministers, or teachers that you listen to on a regular basis for spiritual guidance and encouragement?

3. What biblical figure and/or story can you closely relate to or connect with?

The Rain Is Coming!

(Devotional #34)

I can feel the rain.
It is on the way.
My spirit is full.
Full of hope!
Hope for a pour down.
A flood.

The rain is coming.
A cleansing is around the corning coming
to purity my soul and
to saturate the roots of my foundation.
I can see it in the spirit.
The drought in the natural means nothing.

The rain is coming.
Get ready for a release of rain like never before.
I believe…
I have to believe.
The rain is coming
and, it is coming for me!

Devotional Scripture of Focus

Genesis 27:28 NIV-May God give you heaven's dew and earth's richness—an abundance of grain and new wine.

Isaiah 45:8 NIV-"You heavens above, rain down my righteousness; let the clouds shower it down.

Deuteronomy 11:13-14 NIV-So if you faithfully obey the commands I am giving you today—to love the Lord your God and to serve him with all of your heart and with all of your soul –then I will send rain on your land in its season, both autumn and spring rain, so that you can gather in your gain, new wine, and olive oil.

Theme Term

Overflow

Devotional Discussion Questions

1. After reading devotional piece, what does "the rain is coming" mean to you?

   ┌─────────────────────────────────────┐
   │   │
   │   │
   │   │
   │   │
   └─────────────────────────────────────┘

2. What are some areas in your life where you would like to experience a pour down of rain from God?

   ┌─────────────────────────────────────┐
   │   │
   │   │
   │   │
   │   │
   └─────────────────────────────────────┘

Allowing God to Get the Glory

(Devotional #35)

After all that I have been through …
By no means has life been easy.
I had to allow God to get the glory.
The pain of feeling abused by the world.
Let down by your kin.
And, betrayed by your clique.
I had to allow God to get the glory.

You know that gut wrenching feeling of
being cheated on,
abandoned,
lied on,
or even being the topic of every discussion.
I had to allow God to get the glory.

What about those days where you no
longer love yourself?
Where living in a state of depression
was a way of life?
And a negative self-image became a daily
visiting enemy?
I had to allow God to get the glory.

See, I had to allow this chance because
there was no one else that I could truly
depend on for healing, not even myself.
God's Word says, "...that in all things God
works for the good of those who love him,
who have been called according to his purpose."
So, I wanted to take Him up on His offer.

I had to allow God to get the glory.
Allowing God to get the glory gives
me an opportunity to let go of the pain of
the past, to live in the grace of the present,
and to hold on to plentiful hope for the future.
I had to allow God to get the glory.

Devotional Scriptures of Focus

John 11:40 NIV-Then Jesus said, "Did I not tell you that if you believe, you will see the glory of God?"

1 Corinthians 15:57 NIV-But thanks be to God! He gives us victory through our Lord Jesus Christ.

1 John 5:4 NIV-...for everyone born of God overcomes the world. This is the victory that has overcome the world, even our faith.

Theme Term

Glory

Devotional Discussion Questions

1. Name and write about two situations in which God has received some glory out of your life?

2. How has waiting on The Lord challenged you to grow in life?

3. How has the knowledge of knowing that all things are designed to work together for your good changed your perspective of life?

Let It Go!

(Devotional #36)

Let go of what could have been.
The days that took your joy away.
The people who walked away freely.
The mistakes you made that you can
NEVER re-do.

It is more than okay to relieve yourself
of who you used to be.
It is fine to live in the moment and enjoy
your current reality.
Remember, you have come such a long way
from the good ole bad days

So, let it go!
Stop repeating the memories that keep
re-opening old wounds.
Allow yourself to heal for once.
Stand in your restoration.
For history will not repeat itself.
It's a new day!
Don't miss it because you
just can't let go.

A Book of Strength

Devotional Scriptures of Focus

Philippians 3:13 NIV-Brothers and sisters, I do not consider myself yet to have taken hold of it. But one thing I do: Forgetting what is behind and straining toward what is ahead.

Philippians 4:8 NIV-Finally, brothers and sisters, whatever is true, whatever is noble, whatever is right, whatever is pure, whatever is lovely, whatever is admirable-if anything is excellent or praiseworthy-think about such things. Whatever you have learned or received or heard from me, or seen in me-put it into practice. And the God of peace will be with you.

Proverbs 4:25 NIV-Let your eyes look straight ahead; fix your gaze directly before you.

Isaiah 43:18 NIV-"Forget the former things; do not dwell on the past.

Theme Term

Freedom

Devotional Discussion Questions

1. Do you have difficulty with letting go of certain thoughts?

2. Do you believe that "change" begins in the mind first?

3. Have you ever felt that you have prolonged or hindered your own healing and/or restoration process? If yes, why?

Nothing Wrong

(Devotional #37)

I am being stretched,
pushed and pulled,
strip down,
completely unfolded.

But, I am secure that I did nothing wrong.
My standing still holds a good status.
Yes, I may feel a little lonely.
Formed bonds broken from the right to the left.
Money may be tight.
Weakness many even be coming to the forefront.
Yes, I may question my obedience from time to time
but, I did nothing wrong.

Reaching out for some sort of connection and
stability.
All that is taking place may not feel good.
The discomfort is evident.

However, the pushing, pulling, loss, and varied
emotions are only serving as confirmation to my
spirit that I am in transition
and, soon enough, I will be fully ready to receive my
blessing of greater.
Holding on to the fact that….
I did NOTHING wrong.

Devotional Scriptures of Focus

2 Corinthians 5:17 NIV-Therefore, if anyone is in Christ, the new creation has come: The old has gone, the new is here!

Isaiah 65:17 NIV-"See, I will create new heavens and a new earth. The former things will not be remembered, nor will they come to mind...

Theme Term

Born Again

A Book of Strength

Devotional Discussion Questions

1. Have you ever associated the delay of certain blessings in your life with self-disobedience?

2. How do you recover from the feeling that God may be upset with you and/or that you have done something wrong spiritually?

It's Going To Be Worth It

(Devotional #38)

The worth that is going to be produced
out of the pain, trials, and tears that have
been shed is going to be something special.

My spirit keeps reminding me that my own
personal greater is coming.
It's going to be worth every ounce of warfare that
has come against me.

The Creator of the entire universe, my God, my
Father, my Daddy is behind the scenes creating a
tailored made blessing for his little girl.

I cannot fathom the gifts that are to be revealed unto
me.
But my spirit perceives it.
It's going to be worth it.

This is the type of "worth it" that makes me want to
battle my own personal Goliath repeatedly for the
sole purpose of receiving my prepared reward.

Not only will I be physically, emotionally, and
spiritually ready for what is to come but now, I will

have the character that will enable me to understand, respect, and nurture the
"WORTH" that is about to be bestowed upon me.
It's going to be so worth it!

Devotional Scriptures of Focus

Deuteronomy 28:13 NET-The LORD will make you the head and not the tail, and you will always end up at the top and not the bottom...

Romans 8:28 KJV-And we know that all things work together for the good to them that love God, to them who are the called according to his purpose.

Philippians 4:19 NIV-And my God will meet all your needs according to the riches of his glory in Christ Jesus.

James 1:17 NLT-Whatever is good and perfect is a gift coming down to us from God our Father, who created all the lights in the heavens.

Theme Term

Goodness

Devotional Discussion Questions

1. In your opinion, what is one of the greatest gifts of being a believer of Jesus Christ?

2. What are some of your own personal Goliaths?

3. What are some examples of your own type of "worth it"?

A Letter from the Author

I would like to thank you for taking the time to read *My Victory for God's Glory: A Book of Strength*. It is truly my hope that this devotional will bless your lives in so many different ways.

The obedience and dedication it took to complete this book required a level of growth, stretching and transparency that I have never experienced in my entire life. So, with that being said, my deepest desire is that you are able to hear The Lord speaking through each written line and feel His strength shining through in a unique and loving way.

Be blessed and remember The Lord is always here for His children.

With Joy and Appreciation,

Krystal

Let's Connect

Website:

https://www.followinghisway.com/author_krystal_williams.html

Email: myvictorygodsglory@gmail.com

Following His Way Publishing is a creative collective company that works with a large network of editors, graphic artists and marketing professionals to publish high quality projects for our customers. We seek to empower every author that we serve, whether it be in our end-to-end publishing of their book or providing consultation services providing free resources to assist them with self-publishing. Our ultimate goal is to produce professional products and providing top-notch service 100% of the time.

Interested in learning more? Contact us today at info@followinghisway.com or via telephone at (877) 4-FHWLLC (434-9552).

Visit Us On The Web:
https://www.followinghisway.com/fhw_writing_services.html

Let's connect on Social Media!

@followinghisway

We look forward to serving you!

www.ingramcontent.com/pod-product-compliance
Lightning Source LLC
Chambersburg PA
CBHW020859090426
42736CB00008B/434